W9-BGY-998

This gift is presented for my Fathers Glory
Because
I'm about my Fathers business!

DEDICATION

To my mother… Mary Lee Hamlet…
Thank you for always being in my corner praying.
Abundant life awaits you, my prosperous Warrior and
Kingly sons…
Vaughn and Royal
To my gorgeous grands… Veronica, Kayla, Royal Jr and
Royalty Grace
Its ALL for you!
To Mommy and Dad…Love Lifted Me!

ACKNOWLEDGEMENT

Intimate Family and Friends…Thank You!
Jeffrey, my life love, I faithfully EMERGE with you forever!

It's Time to rise to the next level! Trust God and Let's go! Love, Dr. Rachel

DR. RACHEL HAMLET HEGGINS

EMERGE
AND SEE

DISCOVERING YOUR UNIQUE
LIFE EMPOWERMENT SYSTEM

EMERGE AND SEE
Discovering Your Unique Life Empowerment System
Dr. Rachel Hamlet Heggins
Copyright 2017
All Rights Reserved
Published and printed in the United States of America
No part of this publication may be reproduced, stored in a retrieval system or transmitted in any way by any means, electronic, mechanical, photocopy, recording or totherwise, without prior written consent and permission of the author except as provided by USA copyright law.

Unless otherwise indicated all scriptures are taken from the King James Version of the Bible.
Unless otherwise indicated all definitions are taken from Merriam Webster's Dictionary.

Cover Design/Book Photography/Photography by KPE MEDIA
www.facebook. Com/kpemedia
336-419-5596

Book Formatting by Kate Brady Designs
www.katiebradydesign.com
kbradydesign@gmail.com

CONTENTS

LETTER TO THE READER

DEAR READER:

I am very proud of this little book and the feel of success and the uprise that it offers.

It has helped me to continue being honest with my writing and my voice. And so, I am very excited about the impact it holds for you in your journey with the words on the pages to follow.

It has been great encouraging you as I also encourage me to continue to get up, rise up, and stay up in the sails and winds of life. As well, it has been wonderful feeding you nuggets to strengthen you as you confidently push thru obstacles and move forward in your gifts and talents. But know too, that this has helped me with my own confidence and voice as well.

I strongly urge you to swing into action. Aspire to emerge from stagnancy and flow into your thriving, vibrant place. It is time for you to be happy and free. It is indeed one of the pleasures of life. So don't stop now. Your time to emerge depends on it!

Emerge Life to you,

Dr. Rachel

rachelheggins@gmail.com

www.rachelheggins.com

"The time for shrinking back is past. Learn to thrive!"
—Dr. Rachel

#emergelife

CHAPTER 1

CLOSE YOUR FACE HOLE
LOW SELF-ESTEEM

"Fear brings punishment, but Faith brings you your hope. Choose to believe."

—R. HEGGINS

Low self-esteem stems out of fear. It robs the desire to achieve by taking away permission to accomplish and steals your gift from your mouth and hand by silencing your voice. It can make you think that what you say and feel is unimportant by paralyzing your thoughts and ideas.

I can remember being a 7 year old chatter box sitting in that little wooden back road country church in Sunday School with my friends. We always sat shoulder to shoulder on those short brown wooden benches and enjoyed having the lesson come alive. My mother was the teacher. She was a good teacher because she was creative, energetic, and amazingly original. But she tolerated no noise or talking while she was teaching. Everybody had been talking at one point or another but I was always singled out. "Be quiet Rachel", she would say sternly. When our little Sunday School class would sing, she was fine even if I belted out the song louder than anyone else while I played the piano; nobody cared. But when it was over and I took my seat, if I even whispered (which I did) after she had told me to shut up, she would pinch me and turn the skin and say, "Didn't I tell you to shuddd up?" This scene happened over and over and on many occasions.

Over that year and the followings years into my early teens, I quietly became introverted. I became afraid to talk, fearful to conversate, chatter, or even to whisper in public. I wasn't sure anymore that I even had anything to say. When I did talk in her class or any class for that matter, it wasn't because I wanted to but because I was put on the spot by being called on. I can still remember my hands starting to sweat, my throat feeling dry, and my tongue feeling like it was starting to cling to the roof of my mouth. I refused the feeling to even try to voluntarily speak. I felt like I was on the verge of becoming a mute. The words "SHUT UP" were being etched on the heart of my mind and now I was starting to believe that was what I was supposed to do. Don't talk, don't sing, don't whisper, don't' communicate, don't be heard; just SHUT UP!

Maybe, just maybe what I would be talking about was not important. But, whether it was or not is irrelevant. The point is this; all that pinching and constantly telling me to SHUT UP caused me to develop a terrible fear of being before people because I thought they wouldn't listen to me. Even as a young adult, I felt that my voice was not important so even trying to speak up for myself became stressful. I remember allowing people to say whatever they wanted to me or treat me any kind of way they wanted. Once, as an adult, I was in a store to buy a piece of jewelry. I knew what I wanted and saw it but had trouble expressing it. The sales person (of another persuasion) kept telling me, you ought to get this. It was not what I wanted but because I was void of owning and using my voice freely, I bought it against my will and paid much more than I ever wanted or needed to. I also began to have deep unbelief in my own ability to perform. I can remember being asked to sing a certain song or play a certain piece of music on piano for someone else. I would often refuse because I really felt that I couldn't get thru it. I became more and more timid and quiet from hearing those same two words so much, "Shut Up"! By now, I didn't think I was good enough for people to want to listen to me. My "I can't" loop tape was playing its own song over and over; "you're not good enough, nobody will listen, you're too afraid." That's what I constantly heard in my head. I wanted to say something many times, but I just could not get words to come out of my mouth.

I had an aha moment which helped me to realize my truths. It took me from teenage to young adult years to start realizing that I really **can** speak and sing well. My ability to memorize and recite was really an intricate part of who I really was. So I began to confront my own negative self-talk about what I felt I couldn't do; I confronted the feeling that I would always stumble with my words and that people didn't want to hear what I had to say, also that I didn't have the words to say that people wanted to listen to. But none of that was true. It was really all in my head. My heart believed that I could finish what I started and that I could finish in excellence. My mother's words were just words. Or were they? Oh, I realize her words carried a lot of weight at the time they were spoken over and over to me. I had believed it all. After all, I was just a little girl when it all started but now I was a young adult and I was beginning to make real some decisions on my own. I was beginning to separate the facts from fiction. I was beginning to see how certain memories and the speech which I had babysat in my memory was deeply affecting me negatively. I was also beginning to see that it was ultimately up to me whether I would allow the impact of being told to "Shut Up" continue to infringe on my entire life.

I began to check my life. I was continuously being taken advantage of in regard to duties performed and remuneration. My friends would say, girl, why are you letting people walk on you like a doormat? They are taking advantage of you and your gift. I had to be the one to bring it to a screeching halt. So one warm spring day, I was on my way to play for a special program. I was driving fast because I was running a little behind time. I was passing cars like I was driving on the Autobahn. But something jolted me and I pulled over on the shoulder. Suddenly, I could see how people were asking much and giving little; and I was doing much and accepting meagerly. Poignantly, I began to decide that I could not afford to be led by my past thoughts that had me shut up in an unvoiced prison that was all in my head. So, that day, I made a pact with myself. I decided that I would start to speak up for myself. I would not shut the big hole on my face. I would begin to voice what I expected and what I would obligate to complete up front.

I then nervously drove to the building of the program and walked in with a new found level of confidence. I felt it. It was on me! I felt that I was beginning to come to life. It felt like I had been in a coma and was waking up out of a deep sleep and needed to stretch. I began to embrace the feeling because it was beginning of a process thru which I had to go to become the authentic me. So, when it was time for me to perform, I nervously walked up, took the microphone, talked a few seconds to collect myself and bellowed out my song. I gave the audience what they wanted and deserved; talent thru the real me.

To my amazement, people actually began to listen when I talked, so I decided to use my voice to sing more by singing in a choir as well as accept more engagements. I also began to use my voice to memorize and recite again with enthusiasm. Using my voice to finish what I started was a huge reality. One day during a spring cleaning spree, I was going thru some folders from about 5 years back. To my surprise, I came across some short musical skits that I had started. So, I began to finish them and assisted young people in church to perform them. I also began to memorize and recite whole chapters, articles, and songs. Even when I was scared, I began to realize that I can do it scared because I was committed to somehow become the authentic me. The authentic me had work to do that required me to talk as well as speak up. I was now moving in that positive direction. My times of shrinking to the background were fading. I was learning to thrive.

——EMPOWERMENT——

Seek to become a thriving violet instead of shrinking back or backing away. Move onward to find, love, light, nourishment, and the courage to move forward into your destiny.

If you can relate to that, try this exercise:

Make an acronym using the letters of the word B E L I E V E. Write an encouraging word for each letter. Write the words on your mirror as a reminder to believe in you!

Use the word AGAIN with the following words to make 3 word-sets:

    A.) Try_____
    B.) Be Brave_____
    C.) Love_____

Think of a time when you could have used one of the above word-sets. Write briefly how it would have made the situation better.

_____

_____

_____

_____

_____

_____

_____

_____

_____

_____

_____

_____

_____

_____

_____

_____

_____

_____

_____

_____

_____

"Continue to do better until your better becomes your best!"

—Dr. Rachel

#emergelife

CHAPTER 2

OUT OF THE ASHES
ABANDONMENT

"I will never leave you or forsake you"
—HEBREWS 13:5

Abandoned persons lack confidence in realizing their worth. They don't trust well which can result in failed relationships. The feeling of not being good enough and that nobody likes them is ever present. They come across as being shy but the real truth is that they are afraid of being hurt. It is a thief of their happiness. This issue is rooted in fear.

My father was a strong but quiet man. So quiet he forgot to show love and affection, give affirmation, or motivation. He only said what the Bible said. Strict!

I can't even remember a time that he ever said, "I love you." Yeah well, I guess that's because he never even said it. That's why! He worked as a self employed mechanic. He wore coveralls that were always covered in car grease and dirt from being under vehicles and lying against greasy machinery and tools. When he got home at night, his hand color was unrecognizable as the grease that covered them became the new color; jet black. He had a special product called GOJO that he used to dissolve the grease and cleanse his hands. This cleaner often adhered to the porcelain of the bathroom sink and that made the bathroom sink in our house on Putman St. in WV, a filthy horror! At 6 years old, I would be on my tippy toes to peer over into that sink and was probably thinking, what the devil is that!?

He never showed any affection toward me or any of my six siblings. There were no hugs, kisses goodnight, head pats for good job or even good riddance. We had no bedtime stories, talks at the table and no very few special times spent together. I missed a relationship with a father that was in the family unit but not relational in nature. Oh my! I've been running on fumes all this time! My love tank was empty.

As a child I felt alone, unloved and that nobody really cared about me. That's a terrible feeling for a young child growing up. This caused problems for me to be able to maintain close friendships even into my teen years. I would find myself feeling like a wanderer. I would draw people to me because of my pleasing personality but could not keep them. And I couldn't even say that I knew how.

As a young adult, I blamed myself for every little negative thing. I was secretly unhappy with myself and pushed good people away because of it. I didn't know how to nurture a relationship because I didn't receive nurture as a child. Therefore, my social skills went lacking. Also, I was hurting inside so I was attracting good but also hurting people.

I was still hurting when I attended my father's funeral. I was now married and had two babies. I was doing a little better but still had many unresolved issues. Now I had another issue. My father was dead and we never had a real heart to heart talk. There were some things that I wanted to share with him. I knew he would never dance with me, or give me life advice but at the least, I wanted for him to be proud of me.

This all turned around for me at my father's funeral. His funeral was huge because he was a prominent preacher at that time of his life. People came from far and near; they flew in and drove in cars and also brought buses. The church was filled to capacity, even in the balcony. Ladies wore their biggest and cutest hats with the suit to match. Men were in their best black suits. The choir was singing melodically slow as our family came in. I was wearing sunglasses because my eyes were so swollen and red. Finally we were in our seats in front of the church. The service was very uplifting and the choir was lively.

There were many guests and speakers who shared their last thoughts about their friend and fellow colleague in ministry. My father's best friend came forward to speak. He was a short, astute man from the Massachusetts area. My mind immediately began to wonder about some specific things. Did he know him better than I, his daughter did? What secrets did they share? Did they talk about their back burner desires and unfulfilled dreams? Did they support each other in their losses and triumphs? Did they enjoy belly busting laughs together? Afterall, that is what BFFs do.

Then he spoke using all the regular ministerial jargon interspersed with some personal stories. He mentioned that my father cared about his family. He then moved to the front of the podium and looked straight at me. He said, "Your father left you a special message." A special message was left for me thru his best friend? At his funeral: reeeaaally? What in the world could that be? "Rachel", he said, "You were his favorite. " I boo hooed something terrible upon hearing those words. But now he was already gone. I didn't even have the chance to respond to it or embrace it during his life. He left nothing much after his life and only a trickle from a fracture in death. With all things considered, I actually felt a release. I could let him go.

A big help for me was to develop insight into my own psychology and stop my self-sabotaging behaviors. I was losing too many good people from my life that I really needed. It was like gushing blood from a bad wound, but I couldn't stop the bleeding. I needed healing so I began to search thru Gods Word for answers. Since I didn't have an earthly father, I began to slowly yield more and more of my heart to God's love. His love began to heal it. Unquestionably, I began to realize with real eyes that He **was** my father. He was proud of me and I was pleasing to Him. I then began to find freedom to sing and create platforms for myself and others. I also endeavored to seek out old childhood and teen friends and began to work hard to reconnect. That was a great feeling of being released to be accepted.

Along the healing path, I came to realize that I am so loved; it's like I'm the only one in the world. I started to experience that I am worthy of love and it is really worth the effort that is put into it. I began to find, love, and care deeply for the child within me thru God's agape love and an extended family of a loving, accepting community of people. God realized that my own biological family could not meet the needs that I had so, he placed me with a new mommy, daddy, and family that were able to pour in love so that I could see, feel, and accept unreserved nurturing and unconditional love.

——EMPOWERMENT——

Treat yourself with ease. Shut off all that head noise that is negative. Continue to do better until your better becomes your best. You are loved!

If you can relate to this, try this exercise:

Your words are a commercial, what do they say about the love in your life?

_____

_____

_____

_____

_____

_____

_____

_____

_____

_____

_____

_____

If your answer was negative, rewrite the commercial positively. If it was positive, write the words, I AM LOVED!

_____

_____

_____

_____

_____

_____

_____

_____

_____

_____

_____

_____

Think of a long lost friend and find a way to reconnect. Write their name and a short message of love you could one day share with them.

_____

_____

_____

_____

_____

_____

_____

_____

_____

_____

_____

_____

_____

_____

_____

_____

_____

_____

_____

"*Do not place your value into the hands of others. It does not mean to them what it means to you.*"

—Dr. Rachel

#emergelife

CHAPTER 3

TRASHED TREASURE
REJECTION

*"Rejection doesn't mean you're not good enough,
it means the other person failed to notice what you
have to offer."*

—MARK ARMEND

Rejection may leave feelings of being useless, not good enough, a failure, loser, humiliation and loneliness. There may also be great brain pain that affects thinking and decision making.

Being a first grader in Mrs. Vie's class in Hancock Elementary was the best. She was a great reading teacher and I loved learning the strategies she taught. She was so good that it prompted me to not just read the stories but to also memorize it in its entirety. When I was called upon, I recited it with full expression and enthusiasm. Mrs. Vie ranted and raved over me but my classmates didn't participate in the celebration. So, I quickly went back to my seat feeling stupid and embarrassed and wondering what I had done wrong. I memorized the next story after that but NO MORE. The pain of not being accepted for what I had remarkably done was too great.

My ability to get my need for affirmation met was locked up. Now I was faced with no nurture and no affirmation; a double whamy! The embarrassment and hurt I experienced caused me to think that what I had to offer was not of value. I carried that pain into other areas of my life with it ending in the same challenge. And because my mother was pinching me and telling me to SHUT UP, now I was really feeling that what I had to say did not matter at all.

I finally learned that I should not put my value into the hands of other people because it doesn't mean to them what mean to me, it doesn't carry the same weight and it's sometimes more than they care to bear. So, instead of trying to please others, I decided to just try to perform and try to be at peace with it. I started to believe that facing and letting go of past pain was well worth the rewards it yields over time.

——EMPOWERMENT——

God knows what he is doing even when you get a closed door. When it is time, the door will open and no force of darkness can ever prevent that.

If you can relate to this, try this exercise:

Write briefly how you will focus on getting around one of your hurdles instead of focusing on it.

_____

_____

_____

_____

_____

_____

_____

_____

_____

_____

_____

_____

_____

_____

_____

_____

_____

_____

Make a list of (3) active things you can do while you take the time to sort your feelings out.

a)_____

b)_____

c)_____

Reframe a rejection situation by circling one of the following:

a) They said no.

b) You grew apart.

c) Priorities were different.

d) They didn't like it.

e) Other

"Be willing to search inside your heart!"
—Dr. Rachel

#emergelife

CHAPTER 4

I'M OUTTA HERE
TRAPPED CREATIVITY

"Having obtained help from God,
I continue unto this day."

—ACTS 26:22

Trapped Creativity occurs as a result of having the natural gift/talent stifled. When stifling happens a natural behavior is prevented from being heard, performed and/or seen. That natural behavior can be talking, whispering, singing, strumming, tapping, dancing, etc. The gift/talent is unable to creatively surface because it is systematically suffocating from oppressive situations reducing it to none or curbed use.

Thinking back, I remember when I was about five years old. My whole family of eight was gathered around in the living room after dinner. We were getting settled to sing together. We had a big brown upright piano in our living room and my mother was getting ready to play it. Before she started, I went into the back room and picked up our ole tan acoustic guitar and began strumming to sing. I felt eager and excited about singing in front of my family because we were a family of singers and musicians and it was fun. However, just as I got started, my older, teenaged brother reached forward and pulled down my pajama pants. So, instead of everyone belting out the song with me, they bellowed in laughter at me. But what was so funny about that? I was just a little girl with three thick crazy- looking plaits and a messy bang trying to be on stage in a safe place with my family but instead I was made to feel embarrassed, ashamed and hurt. I didn't think it was funny at all. I was embarrassed, ashamed and hurt. On top of that, no one came to console me, so I ran back into the back room crying and put the guitar away. I felt like I had just been buried alive. I felt like I was suffocating. I cried so hard I could hardly even catch my breath. I didn't want to ever play again. And I didn't even touch one for many years.

The negative effects of being shamed and embarrassed as a young child in front of my family were very strong. I refused to do much of anything before people. I didn't talk, sing or play instruments before people voluntarily. I always had to be coaxed. My parents, teachers and friends had to constantly request, plead, and beg for me to perform and/or participate.

When I was in my middle teens, the shaming and embarrassment incident caused me to turn inward and build a wall. Unbeknownst to me, behind that wall and under that pressure of feeling my gift buried, I was getting paid wages for just being there. It was paying me wages of mental punishment by gagging my voice into silence, emotional punishment by robbing me of my best friendships, and physical punishment by taking away my very appetite for food.

One day while practicing a song that I had heard, I was offered a chance to sing that very song in a play. I blatantly refused the offer, not because I couldn't do it well, but simply because I felt like I might suffocate, black out or just simply stop singing. Even with this missed opportunity, I didn't and couldn't come out from behind the wall or let many people into my life. Not even my family. It just seemed too hard and I didn't have the strength to get up out of that rut after all of that inflicted pain and shame and embarrassment that seemed to cover me. I felt as if I had been buried underneath all that pain, shame and humiliation. Plus, I didn't know how to get out and you just can't do what you just don't know how to do.

As a young woman, I really began to see that I was basically a trap for the gifting inside because when I would sing or perform, people really seemed to enjoy it and always seemed to want more. It was then that I began to realize that there really was creative talent inside me, but it was locked in. I didn't know how to let it out but somehow I was determined to. Having been told to SHUT UP for such a long a time had its lasting effects on me. But I couldn't let it hold me back for the rest of my life. I can remember when I was 19 years old and I sang and played for a solo part in a community choir. I was soooooooo scared just thinking that in 30 days, 2 weeks, and then in 60 seconds I would be on that stage with about 200 sets of eyes on me. The day before, I was so nervous that I couldn't sleep for the fear constantly pressed me. My heart constantly raced, my mouth was dryer than a desert on a hot day. Even my palms were sweating, which was something new I started experiencing. I thought my heart would swell up and burst on the day of the performance. Then it was time.

I slowly moved onto the stage feeling like I had cement in my shoes, my heart pounding in my ears. I looked into the audience and thought to myself, I CANT DO THIS! I then met the eye of the cutest 2 year old that had such affection and anticipation in his eyes. At that split second, I knew that I could perform even in the midst of this huge throng of doubt and nervousness that entrapped me. At that moment, I let myself go by throwing myself totally into the song without thinking about anything but the song. I started singing, "How Do I Get Outta Here"! That SHUT UP syndrome was losing its power over me. That very incident allowed me to grow graciously into womanhood as I began to remove the suffocating dirt of my past that I felt buried beneath. The diamond that I am was emerging and started to do greater things. I was beginning to smell the clean air of freedom and I was beginning to love it.

Releasing the trapped creativity in womanhood is not easy. It took a lot of deep soul searching of my mind and thorough probing of the lies I had allowed myself to believe, and facing my inner fears, uncertainties, and faults. For instance, I still believed that my family hated me and were responsible for me being trapped. I still thought that they would have to untrap me somehow. But they were not responsible for me letting loop tapes play in my head or continuing to believe that I had to forever be SHUT UP. They were not responsible for me being hostage. This was a stronghold and I had given this stronghold permission to stranglehold my thinking. So, I had to come to grips with my own stronghold of fear and walls of defeat and fear of failure. I had to identify the strongholds of my thought life and deal with their grip through the power of prayer and right thinking. I prayed diligently and was fervently prayed for and slowly began to allow my thinking pattern to see differently so that I would know how to renew my mind. Therefore, as the strongholds began to loosen and the fears decreased, I became increasingly focused. I also became increasingly aware of how bound up I had been and that I could never have gotten loosed alone but only with God as my ultimate helper. With Him I realized that I could conquer anything! At last, I began to feel a flood of happiness and peace within because I could finally begin to focus on releasing the trapped creativity and then begin to release the gifting within to bless me and ultimately bless others. Up out of the dirt of my past I began to emerge as a lively, singing and multifaceted woman.

EMPOWERMENT

Be unequivocally willing to search inside your own heart and let go of anything that might hold you back from what you know that you are destined to do. Only then you can mount up and fly like an eagle and soar!

If you can relate to that, try this exercise:

I sometimes think of myself as a product on a store shelf. I am PREGO (It's all in there! What product are you?

Why?

_____

_____

_____

_____

_____

_____

_____

_____

_____

_____

_____

_____

Write the three (3) main things you found that you need to face, deal with or change.

A). _____

B). _____

C). _____

Intentional soul searching Is therapeutic. Be sure to take at least 1 hour a day of reflection.

"God' amazing grace will transform and make connecting moments happen."

—Dr. Rachel

#emergelife

CHAPTER 5

A MAZE IN GRACE
INSECURITY

"Be yourself, everyone else is already taken"
—OSCAR WILDE

I nsecure people often go around in vicious cycles because they are not sure of who they are, and what they believe about themselves. They can be easily manipulated by stronger personalities due to their desire to please others. They don't understand their place in the world and can become easy prey to bullies. Their poor formative experience, chaotic, distressing childhood, adolescence/early adulthood experiences, rigid expectations, fear of someone, lack of setting roots, growing wings because of domestic violence, physical, sexual abuse, can cause specific defense mechanisms. These help protect the barely nourished sense of self from those in power over them. They often have trouble speaking up for themselves and sometimes have problems not valuing self worth greater than their sexuality.

As I moved into adolescence, I began to play and sing more in church, and on different programs, but I could really feel the heaviness of an entrapment and longed to be free to let my spirit soar and perform without the shame and embarrassment in which I was entrapped. As I watched other people perform with confidence, I could feel the freedom of their spirit to own their voice and release the music. I wanted that so bad that I began to search deep inside my heart and ask God to help me with the chaotic recycling and unending maze I was in. I remember when I would sing, how I felt that my voice was singing inside my body instead of outside of it. I needed Him to show me, change me, and give me grace to be released! But there were so many things done to me and I was hating on some people for doing it. Slowly, I began to see that I had a problem with forgiveness and that I also needed to be forgiven. I needed help to forgive my parents for allowing that shameful situation to happen and to also forgive my brother as well as the perpetrator for participating in that awful situation. Only then could I begin to forgive myself for babysitting it all that time in my mind so that the mazes of insecurity could be resolved.

It all makes so much sense that I had felt lost and confused for so many years. When I moved into my 20's, I began to unravel the maze of effects of shame on my life due to the sexual abuse incident. Soooo many unanswered questions, negative effects and unfinished things in my life began to make sense. How about I remembered that I was fondled, molested and treated inappropriately in the basement of my parent's house in WV at 5 yrs. old? My brother called me to come to the basement. I went because he was my brother and I trusted him. When I got there, he told me to go in. I did. There was one very dimly lit bulb in a ceiling socket just inside the door to light the whole area. He told me to go over there. Go over there? Over where because over there was kind of slanted and rocky because the floor was not level. It was dark and damp because there was no real floor. Only original dirty earth and jagged rock was there. Lay down, he told me. Then another boy appeared. He was about nine or ten years old. He charged into me, pulling up my dress and down my panties so fast that I couldn't scream. He was moving his body on me for what seemed like eternity. Then finally he got up. My teenage brother watched the whole thing. My same brother who pulled down my pajama pants set this up and then stood there to watch it!? Now wasn't that just a mess!

That harmful sexual occurrence that I encountered as a very young girl, coupled with very minimal nurture growing up and a very, strict upbringing caused me to experience a sexual identity crisis later in my life as a teen and into early adulthood. I didn't know who I was, how to carry myself, what to feel or think about anything outside of church because my parents were so strict. I was not even allowed to talk to boys outside of our family growing up. We were in church almost every night of the week. We had no television. We were not allowed to participate in many recreational sports, activities and games. My life was almost a blank slate except for the negatives of all the things that I couldn't do and the negative experiences that I had endured in my life. The cycles that the negative experiences took me thru made me feel like a gerbil running on a wheel in a maze. I was constantly going from person to person, trying to be friends; going from grown person to grown person, trying to be nurtured. I didn't even know exactly what all I was looking for, I just knew I kept going in circles and seemingly always meeting myself coming back, instead of a solution.

One of the things I came to realize with real eyes is that my parents did not know how to nurture or love because neither received such for themselves. My history review of my mother shows that her mother died at 31 years old in childbirth. Mother was only 8 years of age and the eldest of 7 siblings. They were taken in by her mother's brother who already had 6 children of his own, of which she was the eldest. She missed going to school many days because of the field hand chores that she had to complete, (i.e. slop hogs, feed chickens, milk cows, etc.). Her school was one room and she was the oldest and biggest child. Growing up, she didn't hear anyone saying, I love you and seldom did anyone hug or kiss her. She grew up just kind of figuring things out on her own by trial and error. This same powerlessness to receive the nurture I needed sent me in a tailspin to find myself, healthy ways to give and receive love, and find the place for my voice in a world that was much different from hers. But just like God's grace kept her, that same grace was with me in my maze of life. That same grace covered me as I reached out to my brother who had watched while I was being molested.

About 15 years ago, I made a spring visit to my gifted, middle brother in his hometown. He looked very manly with his facial hair, straw hat and pressed jeans. We had a chance to sit on his porch in the cool of the evening and reminisce about some of our childhood memories. Our conversation had gone on for about 20 minutes. Then something happened in the middle of the conversation. He suddenly stopped talking and looked at me strangely. He then looked away. Then he asked, "How are you really?" I thought to myself, why is he asking me how am I REEE-AAALLY in the middle of our conversation? I looked at him intently and saw the pain trapped in his face. Wow, he too had carried a burdensome memory. I reached out for his hand, and he reached back as I responded with compassion, I REAALLY am fine now. I saw the hint of a smile. " I love you," he said, without ever even looking back my way. That was his way of saying I'm sorry I suppose. I accepted that. This was an awkward situation for both of us but at least we had created a moment in time for healing to begin. I still didn't understand it but at least I realized that he too was a victim of little nurture. That didn't excuse what he did but it released my heart at this stage of my maturity, to be free

Suddenly, I began to realize that I couldn't blame my mother for what she did not receive and needed her own self. Nor my brother for what he never received from her. So, I decided that I didn't have to become fixed on the past and walk with it as a constant companion. I came to recognize that I needed to stand up and make some things happen for me.

I clearly recall when I signed my own permission slip with my father's name to go on the senior class trip to the water park. I was soooo excited and happy. I borrowed a bathing suit because I didn't own one, and had a lil Mr.Latino boyfriend with his cute freckled face. We sat in the back of the bus and kissed almost all the way there. Once there, he had his arm around me and held my hand as we walked around the park. I was almost in heaven. He knew I was a church girl and that there would not be any bumping and grinding business. He didn't care and you know I certainly didn't either. He liked me and I liked him and that was all that mattered.

I felt good about doing a lil something for myself. I just needed an outlet to be free to let myself grow, improve, and be wiser and stronger. I wanted to make history in my family and be the first to do something greater. I felt the push to leave my family after high school and do something nobody in my family ever did—go to college. But because I was living at home, it was a struggle for me to face getting all the necessary papers signed by my father. So I did what any bodacious but ambitious child would do. Once again, I signed them myself. That part of the maze was solved. I now realized that there was still some strength and courage inside me to live a big circle instead of constantly in a maze.

I have to keep looking at my own strengths; I have to focus and then refocus on them. They always balance out my flaws. So now, there's no need for me to compare myself to other people. In this, I have learned to relax and not worry about the negative that could happen. I can now laugh about the dumb stuff, and not take myself too seriously. After all, nobody is perfect. I have my own imperfections and so does the next person.

I tell myself: I value you; I love my personality, so I

have stopped caring so much about how people perceive me. Now I can begin to just let go and be myself and let my creativity flow. I keep myself around positive people, and trusted friends. I am my own best friend first because I am worthy of love. And because I know I am worthy of love, I can begin to allow my voice to be heard even more because of God's Amazing Grace.

@RachelHeggins

DON'T COMPLAIN ABOUT THE NIGHT OF LIFE. THAT'S WHERE THE BLESSING OF MIRACLES CAN TAKE PLACE!

Dr. Rachel Heggins

W W W . R A C H E L H E G G I N S . C O M

——EMPOWERMENT——

Accept yourself by finding out what you value; what defines you, and what is your essence. You are wonderful so learn to love you so that you can in turn love others! BeYoutiful! R.Heggins

If you can relate to this, try this exercise:

On a scale of 1-10 (10 is the highest) rate your level of self- acceptance.

My level is: _____

Name three things that you most value about yourself.

A._____

B._____

C._____

Take the time to meditate on God's Amazing Grace.
Write any impactful thoughts.

_____

_____

_____

_____

_____

_____

_____

_____

_____

_____

_____

_____

_____

_____

_____

_____

_____

"*The light of God's word will come,
the shadows will disappear, and reveal the beauty
that has been covered.*"

—Dr. Rachel

#emerglife

CHAPTER 6

LONELY MISFIT
LONELINESS

*"...Surely I am with you always, even to
the end of the world."*

—MATTHEW 28:20

L oneliness denotes being without company and friends;
cutoff, disconnected, alienated. There can also be a feeling of being hollow and empty inside. A misfit, on the other
hand is characterized by certain behaviors or attitudes that
uncomfortably sets them apart from others because they
don't fit in! they are courageous to think outside the box and
be different from those around them, in spite of being alienated from the people around them. They are a challenge to
conventional thinkers and make the world interesting, This
issue is rooted in heaviness.

I can remember when I was about four years old, my first
elder brother picked me up and sat me on the old washing
machine on the back porch of our house back in the hills of
WV. I thought my three brothers were gonna play a game with
me but instead the joke was about to be on me. They asked
me to sing a song entitled, RESCUE THE PERISHING,

CARE FOR THE DYING. Well, I was very young and I couldn't enunciate my words quite well. So, I started singing, wiggling my arms and moving my heard back and forth to the beat. It was on, or so I thought. You couldn't tell me I wasn't sounding good aaannd I knew the words! I was just a singing! Reeeeescue the Perishit, Care for the Dying, - what, oh no! Uh…Did you just cuss? NO! Obviously my brothers thought I did and proceeded to ring out in chorus….Maaaa, Meetee (as I was affectionately nicknamed) out here cussin! My mother's response; git in this house girl and go to bed and don't get up 'til I tell you! I was put back down on the porch. Sadly, I walked thru that old wooden screen door, thru the kitchen and into my bedroom; which was shared with my older and younger sibling. I crawled up on your top bunk by stepping on the lower bunk, up onto that ole dresser nearby and then up and over the safety rail. By this time, l was balling my eyes out. My eyes would be blood shot read and swollen from crying so hard. I just didn't understand why I was sent to bed for nothing. I would be there for most of the day because she would forget she sent me there. When I would ask, Ma, can I get up? She would respond, SHUT UP girl. I felt like Joseph (of the Bible) being sent into the dungeon for nothing! I was so alone and cut off from everybody. I could hear my siblings playing outside and having fun in our big yard. They would be playing a tag game or shooting basketballs. It sounded like such fun! Ma, can I get up? SHUT UP girl!

I felt so unloved by my siblings. It seemed they didn't want me around. Was I dreaming dreams and telling them about them? They were being so mean to me for seemingly no reason. I could see it if I was being a real brat. But I wasn't. I was the gifted quiet one. And the gifted quiet one was merely trying to get someone's attention for friendship, nurture, and love at least from my family. As a result of being bullied at home, I was targeted for six years of elementary school. I ran home from school every single day the Lord sent. When the final dismissal bell rang at 2:30p at Hancock Elementary school in WV, and my two little feet struck the pavement outside, you had better speak to me quick, fast and in a hurry because you were about to eat my dust! I had a big sister in the school but I didn't even wait for her. She was always with her friends and taking her time getting home. My few friends would see me again in the morning on the playground, plastered in the corner by the back entrance door. In high school I was still had few friends. I started to think and speak self- defeating thoughts that I seemed to always have in my head. I'm not worthy of friends, I'm not cute enough to hang with the popular people; they're all smarter than me. Feeling like an outcast, I started to venture my aloneness into sports. As a loner I always felt strange. I was alone but somehow not totally unaccompanied. Somehow that strangeness was keeping me company.

I excelled at sports at the high school where we had moved in Connecticut. I had many admirers from a distance but only two for real friends, Ali and Dot. I participated in and excelled in track and field, gymnastics, basketball, softball, volleyball, tennis and other sports. I even dabbled in a few leadership roles in spite of the fact that my parents were against every extracurricular activity I did. Then I suddenly began to realize something. It wasn't just about me and the fact that I was good at whatever I put I hands to. It wasn't even about the fact that they had strict rules that kept me isolated and trapped. But it was totally about the fact that neither of my parents had reached their dream so they didn't even know how to support me to reach mine. They didn't know how to encourage me by cheering me on. They didn't know how to nurture a gift with love and support. They just didn't know. I remember my mother once saying to me when I was a young woman, you know, I always wanted to go back to college. I really thought your father would send me once we got married but I started having babies. That was the end of that dream. She also relayed not long after that, how she used to sing with a travelling singing group. She had to give that up too after she married and began to have babies. In the words of Langston Hughes, I ask: "What happens to a dream deferred"? After seven quick babies, her dream was buried. So I can no longer overreact when I think of what I went thru because when I really I look at what she has carried, I see plainly that she too has felt alone.

The best thing that helped me begin to leave my strange company keeper was to step out of my comfort zone and reach out to others that were also reaching out. I had to find ease even in my time of discomfort to reach out anyway. The best thing that I came to understand is that I had to reach out to my mother and my brother and my siblings. I had to begin to take the focus off of me and what I have been thru and focus on the feelings of others. This helped me to see some of what they too had gone thru and begin to see how they were like me in a lot of ways. Though I realized that I had lost the ability to cultivate and use my voice, now that I knew I could somehow get it back, I was beginning to see how I had the chance to make history right.

I remember as a divorced woman, having a candid talk with my mother about being pinched all the time. Not just pinched, but pinched and then told to SHUT UP! She shared how there were some things going on in her marriage with bills, keeping a roof over us, money shortages, and keeping her marriage together. Those things caused her to often be depressed. Depression can cause anger to rise and spill over on something or somebody else. I was one of those somebody's and my 15 years old brother was the other one. We both are middle children. I am the middle girl and he is the middle boy. Mother said to me, "I'm sorry, I didn't know what to do." She never said, I love you but I accepted what she did say because I really felt that was all she had to give. That very moment in time set the tone for some healing to begin. I felt that strange feeling starting to dissipate. I felt like I was stepping out of a shadow and into light.

——EMPOWERMENT——

Don't be afraid to walk in a shadow. Soon light will come and the shadow will disappear and reveal the beauty that had been covered.

If you can relate to this, try this exercise:

Search the internet and find a group that you share interest with. What is the name of that group?

_____

Join and participate!

Inside of the group, begin a new friendship with someone with whom you have things in common in your new interest group.

Write two (2) of the common things you have.

a)_____

b)_____

Resign from the procrastinators club. Place a reminder to attend in a good place and do it! Where will you put your reminder?

_____

_____

_____

"See yourself living in freedom."
—Dr. Rachel

#emergelife

CHAPTER 7

BREAK OUT!
STRONGHOLDS

*"For the weapons of our warfare are
not carnal, but mighty through God to the
pulling down of strongholds"*

—II CORINTHIANS 10:4

Strongholds make you hold onto faulty thinking patterns that are based on lies and deception. You are kept trapped from God's best because of this way of thinking. They can make you hold onto an unhealthy fear of God. It builds a wall with deception as the biggest building block because it colors perception, kills the life fruit and keeps lives from changing. People dealing with strongholds may have some demonic influence and control, exhibit resistance to change reinforced with subtle argument and pretense of logic against the Bible. Usually you can't hear God.

The four years I spent in undergraduate school was the training ground for handling independent freedom in my life. It was during this time that I began to really find my identity in Christ. I went through a season in my sophomore year where I battled with mild depression and attempted suicide because of all the pressure to balance strict parental influence, school, sports, guys, grades, church, parties, and just college campus life. The most pressing was my strict parental influence. Everything was about church, church, church. Go to church, not to dances, there will be boys and you might damage yourself. I remember how we couldn't go to parties, sports events or movies. So, the college campus became my new life of new freedom but with new guilt. Being a college student was great but all of the rules from my strict parents cramped my college life and sent rivets of its influence into every aspect of my college life. I was always feeling guilty about going to a regular party; I felt guilty if I liked guys because as a youngster we were not allowed to talk to them. So, in college, I had the freedom but I felt guilty in my freedom to even just act my age, be silly sometimes and just have some good ole clean fun.

I didn't pray as much or read my Bible as much in college. The influences around me were great and strong. Most people did not seem to think like me or act like me. I was the "church girl". I was more withdrawn, quiet and basically alone. I had a few friends but I was definitely not a part of the crowd. I needed to find my own identity: who I was as a person and who was I in Christ. I also needed to find the right way to get my basic needs met. My coping skills were very weak to non-existing so the pressure of being on my own to deal with so much coming at me, consumed my strength.

One early spring night, I was feeling so very pressed about finals, my date for the college spring gala, my parents probably not agreeing to it, keeping it secret from them, what would my date think and on and on. I started asking kids on my hall to give me a couple of their pain medicine pills. I was suffering from migraine headaches at that time, so I told them that I just wanted to go to sleep. I ended up with about 6-8 pills. I took them at about 9p at night and lay down. I went to sleep and was awakened to somebody shaking the dickens out of me the next morning at about 11 o'clock. I thought it was people on my hall waking me for a fire. Instead, it was EMT emergency workers trying to get me awake and alert. They were checking my room for drugs and whatever else. I was being questioned about what I had taken. I told them sleeping pills. After much probing, I was dressed and walked to an ambulance for transport to a hospital.

I remember the feeling I had as I left with EMT from my dorm building after the suicide attempt. I was walking so slow that they asked me if I wanted to ride in a wheelchair. I didn't want to ride, I wanted to hide. I was so ashamed and embarrassed to be in that situation. It was like taking a walk of shame down the hall, out the elevator in to the front lobby. Oh no! Not the front lobby! You would think I had set myself on fire or something. People were lined up in bathrobes, pajamas and shorts with tees, curlers, some barefooted and others in slippers; just to get a glimpse of the girl who tried to attempted suicide. If I had a dollar for every stare, I would be pretty rich. I just wanted to run and jump into the back of that ambulance but my legs were like jelly and I was groggy as heck. Finally we got to the ambulance. It took me three tries to get up in there. Whew! Finally I could sit down and be out of that circus I had come thru. I felt so terribly ashamed of myself but I also was wondering ahead about what my strict father was going to say about this situation. After I was evaluated at the first hospital near school, my father drove me to a hospital in my hometown (about 30 minutes away). I was evaluated and sent home. I was sent back to the strict house.

When I was sent back to the strict house, I had time to think, pray and read the Bible. I began to meditate on what I read. I also began to put the truth of God's Word to work in my life by listening, obeying and living it daily. I evaluated my way of thinking about God and found that I was really angry with Him because of my past sexual molestation situation and my parental dysfunctional living situation. I came to realize that I needed to ask God to forgive me and to reconcile my relationship with Him. I also saw that there were some things that I had inherited into my life (passed down through my family generational line): things such as a poverty mindset, low bar thinking, negative thought loitering, carrying the cross of rejection, walking alone, and the confusion of never having been nurtured by my mother. What a big, thick chain that was that had to be broken. Without it broken, I could never reach my potential in life. Those things needed to be broken and released from my life. So, I began to see myself differently. I began to see myself as God sees me: whole, beautiful, gifted, talented, and loved. This misfit woman was finally beginning to find her way and was finding her place. That was the only way that I could ever gain freedom to own my full voice and rise to soar like eagles.

I began to hear Gods voice speak direction and love to me. I began to show humility and humbleness to receive input from others even if I didn't agree. For instance, I had a hard time accepting criticism because I would feel that I was being attacked. But I wasn't being attacked, I was being given constructive criticism so that I could change and smooth out some rough areas.

My sister used to always say to me, girl, stop acting like you know everything. There's always somebody that can help you with something. I would get soooo mad at her. But one day as I was working on a particular line in a song, I hit a wall. KuuuuuhPow… nothing would come. Her little voice came flowing right back in my head…"There's always somebody that can help you with something."

I immediately called a musician friend of mine and explained my musical dead thought zone. He spoke two words to me, that I'll never forget, "Break out" meaning, get out of that durn box of dead thought. Let go of thinking on your words, music, and gift the same way every time. The humility to call him freed me to think, live, and be higher in other aspects of my life: musically, emotionally, socially, physically and especially spiritually. I sang more freely, accepted more appointments to perform, and walked in the action of faith. I especially gained strength to identify my strongholds and began to take steps to break them off of my life as I began to walk deeper in how God loves me; like I'm the only one in the world. And because of that love, I'm beginning to believe I can do anything…I even believe I can fly, oh yes, I can and will soar!

——EMPOWERMENT——

"There has no temptation taken you but such that is common to man: but God is faithful, who will not suffer you to be tempted above that you are able; but will with the temptation also make a way to escape, that you may be able to bear it". 1 Corinthians 10:13

If you can relate to this, try these exercises:

Here is a short chart of stronghold headings,

Insecurity, Worry, Despair, Bitterness, Anger, Self-Pity, Lust, Pride, and Rejection

Now write the 2 that you might need to deal with.

a.)_____

b.)_____

Describe a situation where a stronghold interfered with your progress in life?

_____

_____

_____

_____

_____

_____

_____

Using the space below draw, four small lines and draw a small box. Put a small dot in the box. Imagine that the dot is YOU in the box. Think of a time when you were totally boxed in on all sides with the feeling of no escape! Now redraw the box with an opening or two. Put the dot on the outside of the box. See yourself living in FREEDOM!

"Unless valued, talk is precious wasted breath."
—Dr. Rachel

#emergelife

CHAPTER 8

THE GREAT UNWIND, UNBIND

Unforgiveness

"Without forgiveness, life is governed by
an endless cycle of resentment and retaliation.
—Roberto A.

Divorce is a 3 headed monster for me! It's painful, it affects the divorced, and it wrecks the whole family unit. We were 10 years into the marriage. Things had been going fine, so I thought. We were two kids, a nice house, good jobs, 2 cars and a dog. Life was good.

We turned the marital curve into year 11 of our marriage and the wheels of our ride began to slowly fall off. I began to talk about what I was feeling. We are losing our magic, our communication was off. We were not on the same page with disciplining the children, and the glue that was holding us together was separating. What was that glue anyway that was holding us together? I had so many unanswered questions. His response was always that everything was fine. So, I stopped talking. I was virtually shut down again as if I had been told to shut up. There was no value being given to what I had to say. Unless valued, talk is precious wasted breath. Two years later, he started talking but I wasn't listening.

My mind took me back to when we got engaged. We were two preacher's kids. We were also musicians and college grads, but what we lacked, was being in healthy love. We both had hurting lives. And our pain was beginning to leak into the marriage. I can remember asking God to help me to decide if this was the man for me. So I decided to do something very specific. Wait. What's that thing called that the church people used to say they did? Fleece, yes that. Here's how it works. You ask God for a specific sign in a specific way and within a specific time. Then you wait to see if it comes to pass within that time frame. So, I asked God to let three red cars in a row come down the street while he and I were walking in the street in his neighborhood. It happened while I was visiting his hometown very soon after. Three red cars in a row slowly came past us while we were walking hand in hand in the street and in his neighborhood. When it happened, my fiancé asked if I was ok. He said I looked as if I had seen a ghost. I told him that I was ok and I brushed off that very important event that I had asked for! What a poor choice to make!

I soon rolled right up into that wedding and married him only to find out about five years later that he too had been molested for several years by someone outside of his family. We had birthed two handsome boys into this fractured family before he even shared that bomb. So buried beneath all of that disorder between the two of us, was our hurt. He was hurting and I was hurting. We were like rumbling volcanoes underneath in our own emotions. Our hurt had brought us together. That was our glue. That was our bond, not love. When I wanted to resolve things, he didn't. When he came to me, I too was angry and refused reconciliation.

I honestly tried to be the perfect working, housewife and mother. I cooked, cleaned, planned family vacations, went back to school and even got my masters, opened a counseling Center in my church, paid most of the bills. Then I looked up one day and I was feeling depleted. But why? Simple. I was tired of this one sided relationship. Basically, I had married a depleted man and it was draining the life out of me. I encouraged him to return to get his masters, but he felt I was pushing him too much. I asked him to plan the next vacation and he decided, he didn't want to go anywhere. He was an engineer making close to 100k a year but where was the money going? Looking back? I don't even know and I didn't question it until we moved into a big, dream house and the bills were much bigger. But I still paid most of the bills, bought all of the new furniture and kept the family going. Then I completely burned out. We started arguing sometimes. He started complaining that I was too busy, bossy and dogmatic; too much like my pastor. I thought I was doing what needed to be done to keep us together. Well, regardless, I was sick and tired of carrying him and the family. I needed help and I needed it now!

At our previous house, I had threatened to leave him, hoping that would change his perspective of our relationship. UUUHHH, that meant nothing. At the new house I threatened divorce. UUUUHHH that meant nothing either.

The boys were turning into teenagers and they really needed strong male guidance. UUUUHHH there was nothing said or done.

In the next two years, we had a few long talks on several short road trips about our relationship and he divulged on one that he had never been in love. UUUHHH WHAT? That said EVERYTHING to me. That was the final bomb. I wound the strings of my heart inside. His free ride was coming to a screeching halt. So where the heck had he been? I didn't know. On another occasion he said he didn't love me anymore. I was sooooo angry and got more and more bitterer with each passing day. What? You were never in love? What the hell were you then, in freaking LIKE?

Then the bedroom ordeal came. Do you know how painful it must have been for me as a married woman to be in bed with a husband who said he didn't love me anymore? Anymore? No, it's more like he never really did. Moving his feet when I tried to touch! Turning over when I reached out! But for real though, I was no angel; I retaliated by doing the same back to him sometimes.

We stayed together 17 years and then divorced. I was the one who left the home. It hurt so very bad to be pushed from my children, my comfort, my family, and my home. But what I know is, I might have lost my sanity if I had stayed. This was very traumatic for me.

My body had weakened somewhat as result of the unforgiveness. I was constantly falling and bumping my head or getting hit in the head mainly by basketballs at work. I had a negative mindset about relationships succeeding and achieving success in life. I ate very little because I had almost no appetite. My skin was bumpy and very oily. I was constantly irritably constipated. I was often intensely short in my responses to my family and friends. I felt that abandoned feeling all over again. I felt unloved and unwanted by my husband and estranged from my few friends.

I was angry and bitter inside because I was losing the one family unit that I felt real connection to. I was losing the family that I had built for myself because I never had that closeness before. Shucks, I didn't even want to date because I felt I couldn't trust another man with my heart or just maybe he wouldn't value me as a beautiful human being. Lastly, I felt so darn guilty for not staying with my teenage boys. I wanted the chance to just be with them whenever they needed me and to share in their love. So, I felt it would be a cold day in hell before I would ever forgive him and some days I even wished that he would just die. But living in unforgiveness is a PRISON. Your life is dictated and your choices are affected. I had chosen not to forgive. I was putting myself in the place of GOD.

As a young married woman who was about to be divorced, I could suddenly see what I was guilty of. I had broken my vows that I had spoken before God just as much as he had. So cried and prayed then prayed and cried. I was so confused about whether to go or stay; whether to leave my teen boys or take them with me. Where would I live, and how would I fare being between jobs? I talked to some friends who could not advise me. Then I talked to the church minister and finally, I turned and began to heartily talk to God. He allowed me to see that I had to decide to I live my life in freedom from the bondage to my own mind. I began to realize how I needed to forgive in order to drop the dead weight of unforgiveness that I carried. Afterall, who was I NOT to forgive? He required it just as much as I needed it.

A few months after I had completely left the house, I heard God tell me to go back and apologize to him. What? Let me check my hearing because surely I didn't hear that. I grappled with the thought for a few days then I called him on the phone. He was cordial and agreed to meet me over food. We had a good talk. Not completely wide, get down and dirty, and tell it all kind of open. But open enough for me to honestly apologize for what I did, said and thought. I didn't get an apology in return. But it didn't even matter because I had done what God told me to do and I felt clear to move forward, climb through this ordeal and live my life with further release from my entrapped creativity and the release of my own my voice.

I began to eat more as my appetite returned. I used to get loud and blast people when I got angry or talked but forgiveness changed all that. My temperament began to neutralize. This whole process of forgiveness gave consent to that hot valve of inward anger to be released and set me free as I acknowledged that ultimately God is in control of my life, not just me. I realized that I no longer had to be bound by strongholds of distancing, coldness, bitterness and a false sense of superiority. I began to walk in forgiveness as a lifestyle and further experienced the climb to freedom in spirit to release creativity and begin to fully own my voice.

When I embraced forgiveness, I received deep peace, good health, and happiness. I caught hold of hope, gratitude and joy because of an exchange. I not only learned to forgive others but I also offered forgiveness to myself and I accepted it through God's grace. The freedom released me to write original songs, and then accept the opportunity go into a studio to work on releasing a piece of it to the world.

——EMPOWERMENT——

"It doesn't really matter if the person who hurt you deserves to be forgiven. Forgiveness is a gift you give yourself. You have things to do and you want to move on".
—Real Live Preacher

"There's no revenge so complete as forgiveness."
—Josh Billings

If you can relate to that story, try this exercise:

Forgiveness is a commitment to change. My level of commitment is still 100%.

At what level of commitment are you willing to work in order to walk in forgiveness?

_____

_____

_____

_____

_____

Write down the names of two people who have offended you that you will actively choose to forgive.

A)._____

B)._____

Write the three (3) main ways in which the above situations had power over you or your life. (voice, health, relationships, etc.)

1. _____

2. _____

3. _____

"Find the source of strength to finally emerge!"
—Dr. Rachel

#emergelife

CHAPTER 9

INCREDIBLE FREEDOM
SHIFT

"Be transformed by renewing your mind..."
—ROMANS 22:12

Transformation can be hard. It is a process that requires major resolution, alteration and conversion. The progression induces change by using all of our cognitive capabilities. The cognitive capabilities are our thoughts, ideas, images, and beliefs, experience. These can provoke a revolutionizing positive shift in thinking patterns, actions, appearance and experiences by thinking on good things, prayer, memorization, the reading of wholesome material, and the Bible. There can be received thru the mind, so many harmful images and experiences of sensuality, anger, and chaos in the course of a day, and over a life's span of time. However, positive transformation can still occur but only thru a major mind renewal. Renewal denotes that a restorative, regenerational restitution will be seen usually over time as the mind adjusts to a new pattern of upgrade.

After experiencing molestation as a child, the heavy baggage of unbelievable shame that comes with that experience, the identity crisis of being a misfit in pubescence and early young adult years, I was in need of a total make over. Early in my marriage, as I sat over a cup of tea in early morning meditation, my life literally began to flash before my eyes. I had accomplished many "things" in life; finished school with your masters (check), got married (check), had 2 handsome sons (check), bought a beautiful house(check), both had good jobs (check), and we went to church (check). Even with all of that list checking, I was still missing something. But what the devil was it? I sat and pondered about how I constantly shrank away with low self-esteem, insecurity, humiliation, and crushed confidence because of the stifling of my voice and the lack of a strong innergame. I then reflected on how I lived under a shroud of shame, low self-worth , pain, rejection, feelings of abandonment, and unforgiveness, because of not knowing who I was, where I really fit in life , and how I would ever have real freedom and love to move into what I was destined to be.

One important thing I began to realize about my life was that I had blinders on that I had grown accustomed to as a child. I was blinded to my own real beauty. I couldn't the inner beauty, charm, good character, charisma, musical gifts, ability to set others at ease, caring, kind, giving and loving ways, humbleness, motivational talent, great listening skills, brilliance, or strong faith. My perception of the real me was covered by all negatives. All I could see was the negative issues with which I struggled. I realized I was trapped in yesterday's anomalously odd normal.

Then I remembered a passage that jarred my stinking

thinking. It says, "As you think in your heart, so are you."
WOW! This gave me another passageway! Like a ton of bricks,
it hit me! The light came on in my pitch dark brain. I had a
SUDDENLY moment. I now knew what I needed. I was in
a metamorphic experience. I was already in PITCH BLACK
DARKNESS in almost every area of my life, so now I needed
to imagine LIGHT until it manifested. Then it happened.

I was playing the keyboard for a women's conference and
the conference host saw my heart. She immediately attached
herself to me but I didn't know it. I was unable to see it
because I was not looking for it. Then one day we spoke
outside of the conference setting. I was then able to hear her
heart. It was a divine destiny moment. It was a joining that
was meant to be. The connection between us was pure and
deeply rooted in God's love. She accepted me as I was. Hurts,
wounds, half-nurtured, and fancy free. Unconditionally, she
and her husband took me into as their very own family.

This was a God set-up that allowed me to be immersed
me into this loving family with an unconditional loving mom
and dad. There I was nurtured and experienced how to love
without limits by being an intimate part of holiday, birthday,
special, and just because celebrations. I learned to give and
receive cards and gifts, and to love who I was becoming and
who I am chosen to be. Thus the next phase of my metamorphosis began.

Slowly, I began to emerge from the life of timidity and
shame. I started to demonstrate the courage to speak to and
in front of young people and adults alike. The divorce was
behind me now. Forgiveness was my gift to what we were. My

guilt regarding my children was gone because our relationships began to flourish again. I also started to leap in my spirit as the music of song voluminously began to arise once again.

Embracing that my tragedies and triumphs would further strengthen areas of my redevelopment, I began to realize how a deeper foundation of truth was being laid by God's Word, prayer and obedience to walk in it. The struggles and soaring would serve as further stepping stones for me and my assignments as well as for others to see and believe. It all gives me confidence, spurs my passion and unleashes boldness as it strengthens my will to succeed. You know, after all I've been thru, struggled thru, suffered thru and endured, I need somebody to know that I am better, wiser, and so much stronger and you can be that way too! But overcoming them was not an overnight ordeal. It took sweat, tears, and a throw down fist fight with my mind.

Finally, I had a briefing with myself and I want you (the reader) to hear it. The briefing went like this. Sister Girl, you are beautiful. Even though you have dealt with a lot of your pain, wrong treatment, rejection, ignorance, stupidity, your own pride, arrogance and stubbornness, there's still some mess in there. Oh, you ain't perfect chile. But you're so much better and your destiny is before you. Your call is answered. All you went thru was for this moment in time. So say goodbye, adios, sayonara, arrivederci, and also THANK YOU to your past with roses and candy. You experienced much of this to keep you sanely grounded, and to show what was really in your heart toward God. You looked at it for what it was and came to a decision to keep it or cast it, walk with it or walk way, save it or stave it. If you're not an asset you're a liability and got to go!

And the verdict is…. You Upgraded! You made it thru the metamorphosis! You are amazing! So now you are safe, whole again, and OH SO LOVED. God loves you like you're the only one in the world! My, my, and you are so gifted and talented it's a God delight! And it's also so nice to know that God is gonna use ALL of your gifts and talents for His glory. People need what you have to give; they need you and the message that you will carry to the nations. You have a voice and you have something to say. So, speak it with boldness, passion, and clarity and they will listen and respond. It's your turn and the spotlight is about to be on you! I say to you (my readers); Come along with me as you work on your own innergame because you too can soar.

Let's go and mount up with wings like eagles... (In my mommy's words), SOAR baby, SOAR ......(In my dad's words) because you're a CHAMPION....GOD'S CHAMPION. You have emerged.

DR.
RACHEL
HEGGINS

LIFE IS A BLANK
CHECK AT BIRTH.
WRITE IT BIG.
SPEND IT WELL.

RACHELHEGGINS.COM   @DRRACHELHEGGINS

——EMPOWERMENT——

Never let what you been through dictate what you're coming into. Just revolutionize your mind and you will see it!

If you can relate to this story, try these exercises:

If you could peek into the door of your heart, what are the two worse things you would see?

1. _____

2. _____

Looking into that same door, what are the two best things you can see?

1. _____

2. _____

It's a brand new day for you. What can you see emerging in your life today?

_____
_____
_____
_____
_____
_____
_____
_____
_____
_____
_____
_____
_____
_____
_____
_____
_____
_____

LIVING
THAT
EMERGED
LIFE
APPLICATIONS

DR. RACHEL **HEGGINS**

I CHARGE THAT YOU ARE QUALIFIED FOR YOUR NEXT LEVEL. NOW GO GET IT!

RACHELHEGGINS.COM

@DRRACHELHEGGINS

CHAPTER 10

CLOSE YOUR
FACE HOLE

B eing told to SHUT UP repeatedly up to my youth years initially took a toll on my communication skills. However, in the interim my listening skills sharpened. It made me hear what others were not saying and what was hidden /missing between the lines.

Consider this:

If you can identify with being told to shut up or some other negative directive, then go back and see how you were strengthened in another area that may be parallel to it or maybe the opposite. (ex. told to SIT DOWN, how you now stand up for yourself…)

_____

_____

_____

_____

_____

_____

_____

_____

_____

_____

_____

_____

_____

_____

_____

_____

_____

_____

_____

_____

_____

_____

_____

_____

_____

_____

_____

_____

CHAPTER 11

OUT OF
THE ASHES

There is something almost surreal about finding and accepting love after dealing with the feelings of abandonment. The fulfillment is unparalleled in kind. But getting to the root of fear left me bearing many scars that are mere reminders of how blessed I am to have faith to believe in change. I had to permit ME to think changed before I could actually emerge into living an emerged life.

Consider this:

Remember the place where you were when you felt that grip of fear while in that abandoned place of your life. (ex. it could be the place of employment loss, loss thru death, family or personal situation).

What was the turning moment which changed your thinking and allowed you to release the grip of fear and grasp the hope of love by faith. If you have not reached this moment, then I invite you to write honestly about what is holding you back. Then really look at it for what it is NOT doing for you.

CHAPTER 12

TRASHED TREASURED

I can still slightly imagine how my life felt when it seemed to wreak with the smell of trash in the eyes of some of the people of my life. Many times I felt balled up and thrown away for years because I felt no one saw me, understood or regarded the value in my life. However, the real problem was not "them", it was ME. I had to remove the blinders from my heart and see ME as GOD sees me; beautiful, conqueror, the head, favored.

Consider this:

Life can send storms your way that challenge your very being to the core. It is so easy to blame others for the things that are designed to make us better at who we are with ourselves. People can makes us feel a certain way but they do not have the resolution to our treacherous times: only God does. So, search within and see those things that have remained constant within you. Build on that. Focus more on what is working than what is not. As you do, you will begin to see the tiny candle light in the midst of your bonfire. You will hear the whisper in the forest instead of the loud voices. God is there. Now write about how who you really are and ways to walk into it by faith.

CHAPTER 13

OUTTA HERE

Ever felt like something had a choke hold grip on your creative talent? The choker is not an outside force. Mine was what I had allowed to grab a hold of me. It was rocking my creative world and leaving me silent in my suffering. I broke the grip by coming face to face with the confusion that was controlling me. I worked hard and diligently to find and get into that place of peace in who I am and my ability to demonstrate in performance.

Consider this:

It's easy to go with the flow but if your flow is negative, there is no growth and therefore you cannot emerge into your area of creativity.

Identify your area of creativity that is trapped? (ex. cutting and styling hair, artwork, dancing, singing, writing, etc.). How can a place of peace be yours in mind, body, and spirit so that your creative juices can flow?

_____

_____

_____

CHAPTER 14

A MAZE IN GRACE

Circles are endless. Mazes offer that same type of circular propensity. Life circles work the same; it's all about patterns.

I realized just how much I was in a life maze when I continued to return to the same spot over and over again. There was no progress and my life pattern was spiraling into walls of nowhere. What helped me to move forward was my desire to see farther and do better. That helped me to focus and become consistent inn strategy.

Consider this:

If you are continually running around in circles or hitting barriers, it's time to stop the circling, get focused and emerge into the next phase of your life. Sit quietly and allow yourself to see and realize the life pattern that has you trapped. Once you see it and realize it, you can stop the pattern and create a new one. Write the things you know are negative patterns in your life. For each negative one, create a new pattern.

_____

_____

_____

_____

_____

_____

_____

_____

_____

_____

_____

_____

_____

_____

_____

_____

_____

_____

_____

_____

_____

_____

_____

_____

CHAPTER 15

LONELY MISFIT

It's a hard situation when the name of the best friend you have as company is that feeling called loneliness. Statistics say, this is called the "age of loneliness." It also relates that 1 in 5 Americans suffer from persistent loneliness even with social media "connections".

When you are lonely and you don't fit into the groups that you feel drawn to presents a whole set of challenges of its own. Forcing friendships is almost like asking for a stab in the back. You end up paying for it, being controlled by it or forced to abandon it because of unfair treatment.

I was like a square in a round hole everywhere I went. I didn't know my value and worth. One huge thing I learned is that some people can see it on you and will use it quickly as an opportunity for their advantage rather than open a door for us to emerge.

Consider this:

Who are you and what value do you bring to the world? Who told you that you are nothing, would never be anything, etc.? Have a conversation around that saying and reframe that feeling until you are sure you are who you say that you are. Remember, you are fearfully and wonderfully made!

Write your thoughts as you begin to process this journey out:

_____

_____

_____

_____

_____

_____

_____

_____

_____

_____

_____

_____

_____

_____

_____

_____

_____

_____

_____

_____

CHAPTER 16

BREAK OUT

There are two ordinary words that when put together can deliver a lot of power. These 2 words can melt hard hearts, mend relationships, bring lives closer together, and squash pride. Those two words are; forgive me.

There have been times in my life where I had to say those words in order to maintain peace, and drop my pride that divides. I learned to say those words with conviction to keep my family relationships together. Family is important to me and I realize that sometimes we have to do what we have to do to maintain closeness and love. Somebody has to emerge out stubbornness and rebellion in order to begin to live in love.

Consider this:

Love is the ultimate goal of life. There are many things that can hold us back from it. Most often we know what those things are but become too afraid or too stubborn to change. But please know that change can transform your whole life.

Write honestly about what those things are and what your intentions are to change them so that you can emerge to the love.

CHAPTER 17

UNWIND UNBIND

I t can be so easy to stay in a loveless marriage, friendship or relationship for reasons such as convenience, comfort, etc. But statistics say that the main reason we stay is this one rubber at the road reason; "I don't want to be alone." That was me in my early friendships and relationships. I was afraid to cut the cord and say goodbye for fear of dreaded aloneness. However, once I relinquished my determination to rely on myself rather than on the strength of God and support others, I became strong again but a different kind of strong. The kind that considers others but most of all allows me to love me.

Consider this:

There seems to be few people who enjoy being totally alone. But even they seem to find comfort in being in the midst of others periodically while dining, walking, biking, etc. Check your personal situation. If you are still there, are you there for the right reasons? Are your emotions there? What kind of emotions are actually there? If you stay will it make you better? If you left, would it make you worse? The main objective seems to be for us to unwind stifling cords that are not love. What cords are binding you? What exchanges do you need to think through that would best free your life to receive love? That's the bottom line. So now, what will you do?

_____

_____

_____

_____

_____

_____

_____

_____

_____

_____

_____

_____

_____

_____

_____

_____

_____

_____

_____

_____

_____

CHAPTER 18

INCREDIBLE FREEDOM

Seeing and needing a major life change is scary. Allowing it to flow into your life can be a paralyzing moment. However, major change can bring a much needed makeover or cause a great emerging upgrade. Refusing or procrastinating change causes stagnation of life and keeps us from emerging into the freedom of life and love. My entire struggle to be free to live and love with no limits came as I released control of me to God and allowed Him to direct my steps. I had many plans for me but I always took myself in the wrong direction. God's plan for me released me from my fear and built my rust to believe He knows what's best for me and has my best interest at heart.

Consider this:

When was the last time you asked God what you should do and which way should you go? When was the last time you checked your living and love level? How open are you for God to intervene and change your plans to what He has in store for you so that you begin to live limitless instead of limited. It's time to live free.

_____

_____

_____

_____

_____

_____

_____

_____

_____

_____

_____

_____

_____

_____

_____

_____

_____

_____

_____

_____

_____

_____

ABOUT THE AUTHOR

Meet Dr. Rachel Heggins. An extraordinarily creative, artistic and motivating force. Such high energy, so bubbly, sweet, humble, and a great magnetic personality. These are just a few precious attributes that she possesses. She wears a coat of many, talents. She was anointed to play piano by ear at 2 years old and released her single debut CD, Holy Are You in 2014. She is a 15 yr. licensed Pastoral Counselor and uses her skill to help transform the lives of private citizens as well as veterans through government contracts. She teaches Physical Education and coaches' high school Track and Volleyball in urban Baltimore City as a means to impact the next generation of entrepreneurs and leaders. She also actively participates in Fellowship of Christian Athletes and with an international women's group called AGLOW.

One would never know that this vivaciously energetic little woman has endured hardships as severe as surviving a suicide attempt to a period of living in her car. Her life is a testimony of God's grace. In spite of these and much more, this woman of God has dedicated her life to igniting other women to act on the emergency to emerge. If you have ever felt like you have not found the treasure in you then it's your time to emerge like an eagle into a champion life.

Dr. Rachel uses simple tools that strengthen the inner game (decrease self- doubt and fear, and increase confidence and find your voice). She then pushes them to emerge and soar. She continues to touch the lives of all she comes in contact with though her music and her life. She is blessed to have ministered on many platforms around the country and abroad. Her unique gifting's are a blessing to all.

In spring 2016, she authored her first workbook; #EMERGE-N-CY. This workbook is a prolific distinctive model that is designed to help you Discover your Voice, Untrap Creativity and Thrive. It allows you to place yourself into the issues presented so that is easier to bring resolution to your own.

She loves to swim, travel, eat fresh, love on her family, teach, pray and witness transformation in those with whom she works. She would love to work with you!

Contact her across social media:
Email: drrachelheggins@gmail.com
Twitter: @drrachelheggins
Facebook: @drrachel heggins
Instagram: @drrachelheggins
Linkedin: @drrachelheggins

48386289R00061

Made in the USA
Middletown, DE
18 September 2017